UKULELE

LEAN ON ME
Songs of Unity, Courage & Hope

ISBN 978-1-70510-544-3

Visit Hal Leonard Online at
www.halleonard.com

Contact us:
Hal Leonard
7777 West Bluemound Road
Milwaukee, WI 53213
Email: info@halleonard.com

In Europe, contact:
Hal Leonard Europe Limited
42 Wigmore Street
Marylebone, London, W1U 2RN
Email: info@halleonardeurope.com

In Australia, contact:
Hal Leonard Australia Pty. Ltd.
4 Lentara Court
Cheltenham, Victoria, 3192 Australia
Email: info@halleonard.com.au

CONTENTS

At the Same Time

Words and Music by Ann Hampton Callaway

First note

Verse
Moderate Ballad

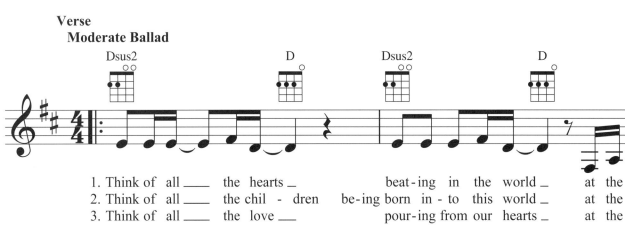

1. Think of all ___ the hearts ___ beat-ing in the world ___ at the
2. Think of all ___ the chil - dren be-ing born in - to this world ___ at the
3. Think of all ___ the love ___ pour-ing from our hearts ___ at the

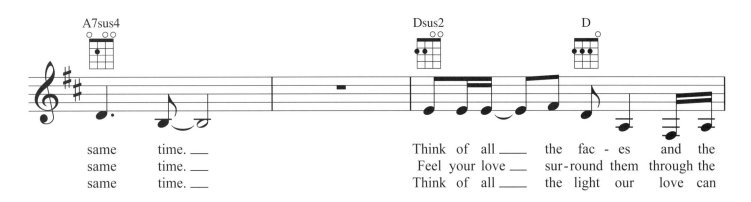

same time. ___
same time. ___
same time. ___

Think of all ___ the fac - es and the
Feel your love ___ sur-round them through the
Think of all ___ the light our love can

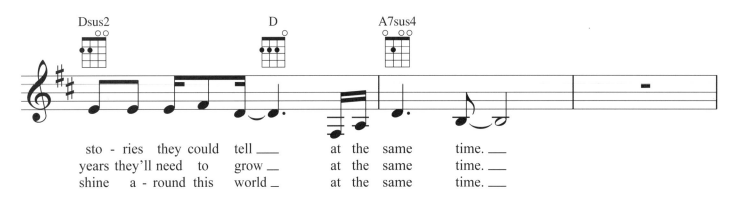

sto - ries they could tell ___ at the same time. ___
years they'll need to grow ___ at the same time. ___
shine a - round this world ___ at the same time. ___

Think of all ___ the eyes ___ look-ing out ___ in - to ___ this world, ___
Think of all ___ the hands ___ that will be reach-ing for ___ a dream. ___
Think what we've ___ been giv - en and then think what we ___ could lose. ___

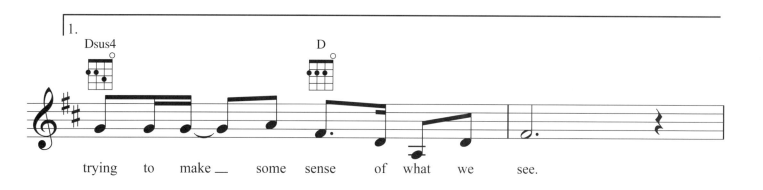

1.

trying to make — some sense of what we see.

Think of all — the ways — we have — of see - ing.

Think of all — the ways — there are — of be - ing.

2., 3.

Think of all — the dreams that could come true —
All of life — is in our trem - bling hands. —
It's time to

To Coda ⊕

if the hands — we're reach - ing with — could come to-geth - er, join - ing me and
o - ver-come — our fears and join — to

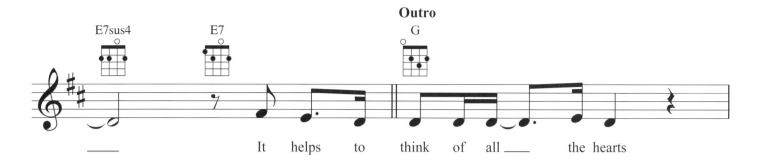

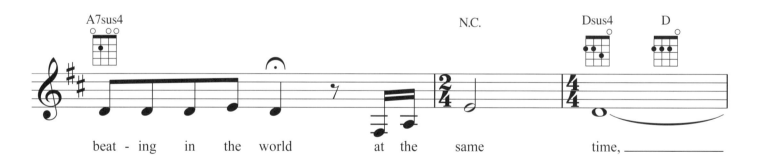

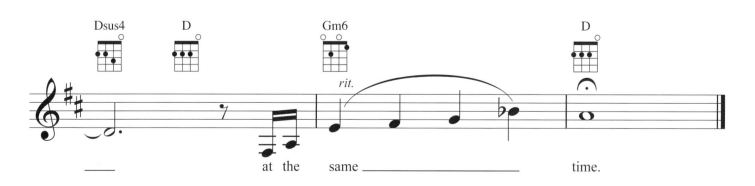

Better Days

Words and Music by Ryan Tedder, Brent Kutzle and John Nathaniel

Verse

up in Cal - i - for - nia, ___ but these clouds, they won't go a - way. ___ Ev - 'ry
up ___ to a new year; ___ got the past a mil - lion miles a - way. ___ I've been wak - ing

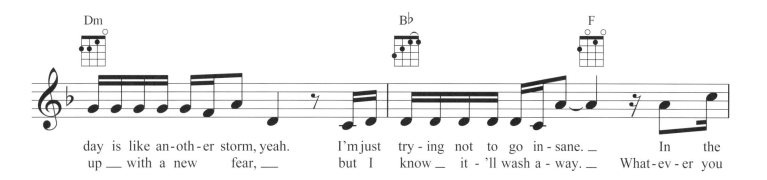

day is like an - oth - er storm, yeah. I'm just try - ing not to go in - sane. ___ In the
up ___ with a new fear, ___ but I know ___ it - 'll wash a - way. ___ What - ev - er you

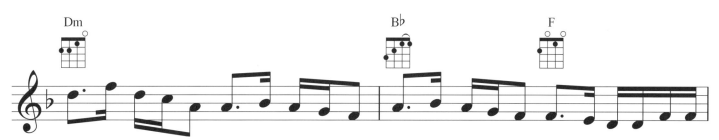

cit - y shin - ing so bright, so man - y dark nights, so man - y dark days. But an - y - time I
do, don't wor - ry 'bout me. I'm think - ing 'bout you, don't wor - ry 'bout us. 'Cause in the

2nd time,
D.C. al Coda

feel the par - a - noi - a, ___ I close my eyes and I pray.
morn - ing, ev - 'ry - thing can change, yeah, and time will tell you it does.

$\oplus$ **Coda**   **Bridge**

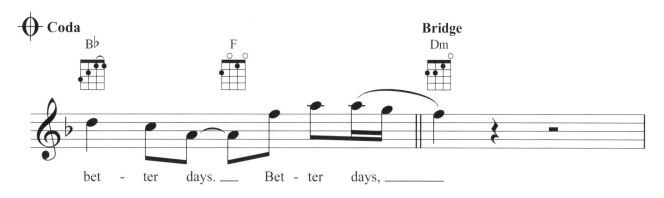

bet - ter days. ___ Bet - ter days, ___

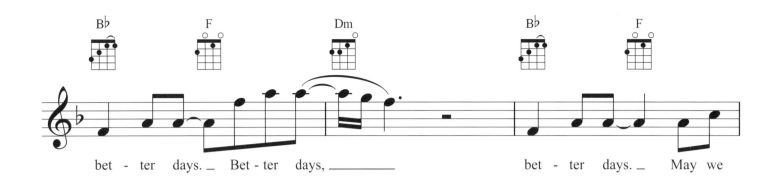

bet - ter days. _ Bet - ter days, _____ bet - ter days. _ May we

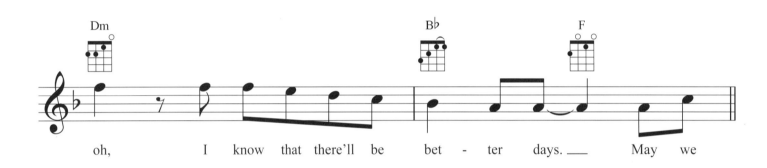

nev - er, ev - er shed an - oth - er tear for to - day, _____ 'cause,

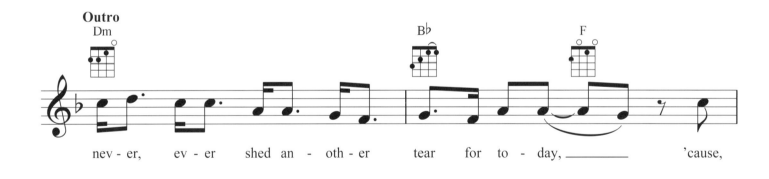

oh, I know that there'll be bet - ter days. __ May we

Outro

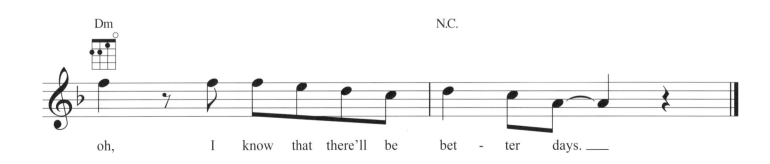

nev - er, ev - er shed an - oth - er tear for to - day, _____ 'cause,

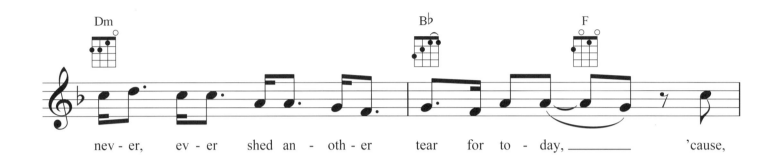

oh, I know that there'll be bet - ter days. __

From a Distance

Words and Music by Julie Gold

First note

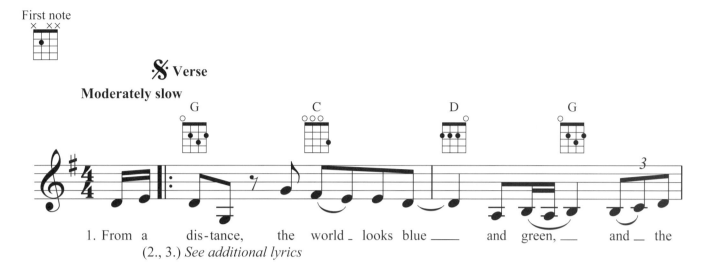

Verse

Moderately slow

1. From a dis-tance, the world looks blue and green, and the
(2., 3.) *See additional lyrics*

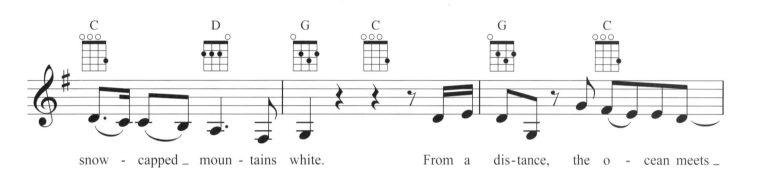

snow - capped mountains white. From a dis-tance, the o - cean meets

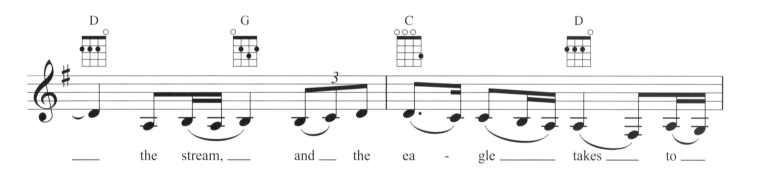

the stream, and the ea - gle takes to

Chorus

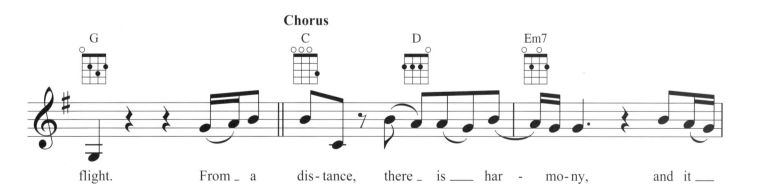

flight. From a dis-tance, there is har - mo-ny, and it

Additional Lyrics

2. From a distance, we all have enough,
   And no one is in need.
   And there are no guns, no bombs and no disease,
   No hungry mouths to feed.

Chorus: From a distance, we are instruments,
   Marching in a common band,
   Playing songs of hope, playing songs of peace.
   They're the songs of ev'ry man.

3. From a distance, you look like my friend,
   Even though we are at war.
   From a distance, I just cannot comprehend
   What all this fighting is for.

Chorus: From a distance, there is harmony,
   And it echoes through the land.
   It's the hope of hopes, it's the love of loves,
   It's the heart of ev'ry man.

Count on Me

Words and Music by Bruno Mars, Ari Levine and Philip Lawrence

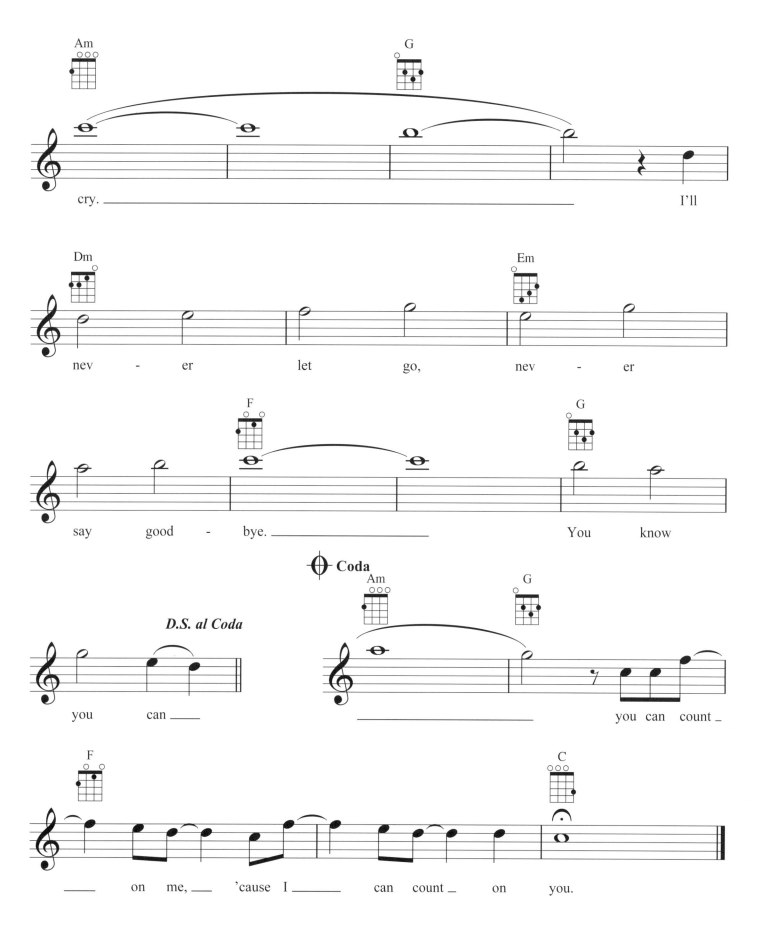

Additional Lyrics

2. If you're tossin' and you're turnin'
   And you just can't fall asleep,
   I'll sing a song beside you.
   And if you ever forget how much
   You really mean to me,
   Ev'ry day I will remind you.

Ebony and Ivory

Words and Music by Paul McCartney

Heal the World

Written and Composed by Michael Jackson

Fight Song

Words and Music by Rachel Platten and Dave Bassett

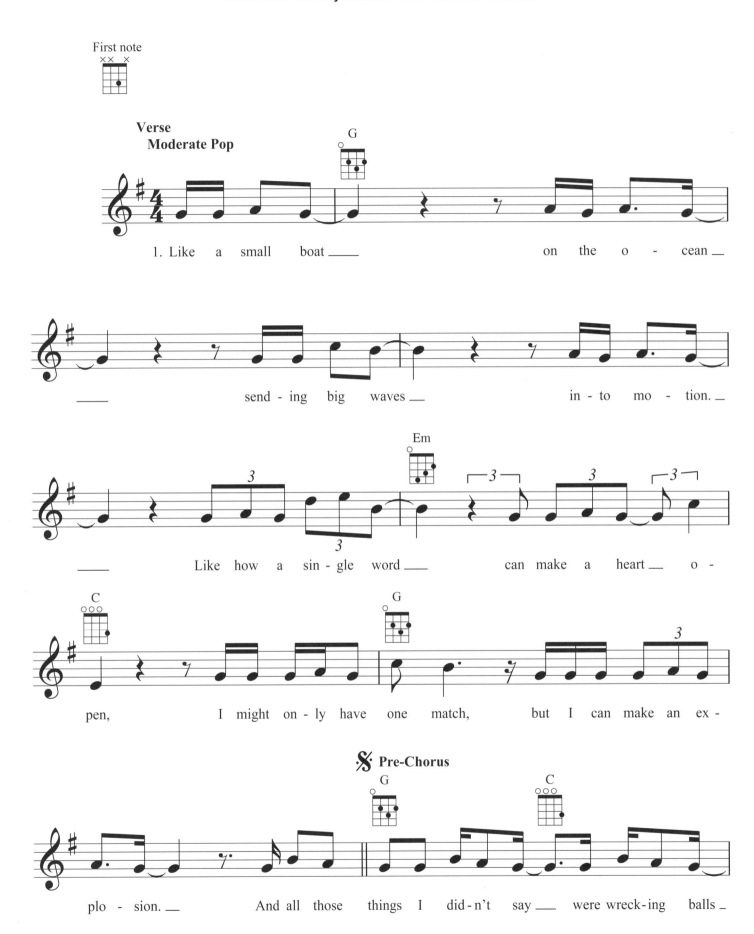

_____ in-side ___ my brain, ___ and I will scream _ 'em a-loud to-night. _ Can you hear _

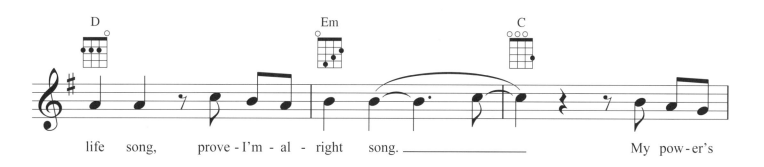

Chorus

_____ my voice _ this time? This is my fight song, take-back-my-

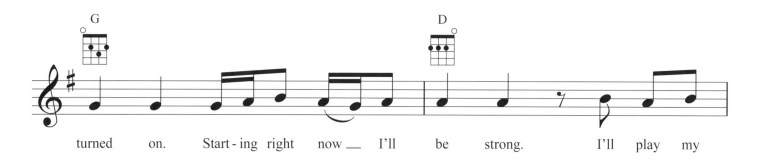

life song, prove-I'm-al-right song. _____ My pow-er's

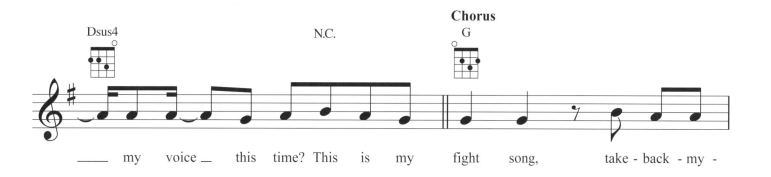

turned on. Start-ing right now ___ I'll be strong. I'll play my

fight song. And I don't real-ly care if no-bod-y else be-

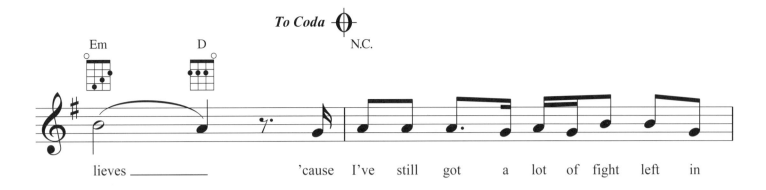

lieves _____ 'cause I've still got a lot of fight left in

Bridge

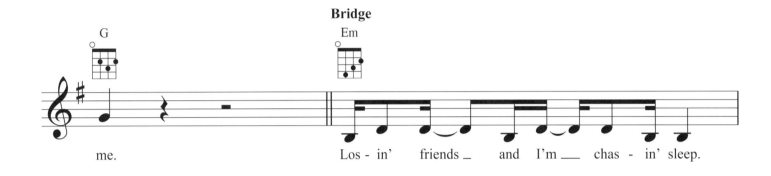

me. Los - in' friends ___ and I'm ___ chas - in' sleep.

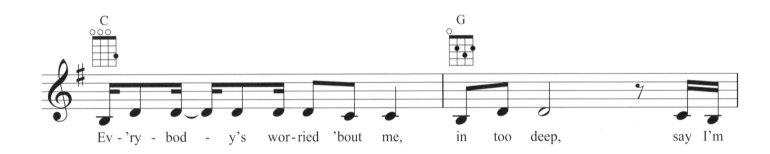

Ev - 'ry - bod - y's wor - ried 'bout me, in too deep, say I'm

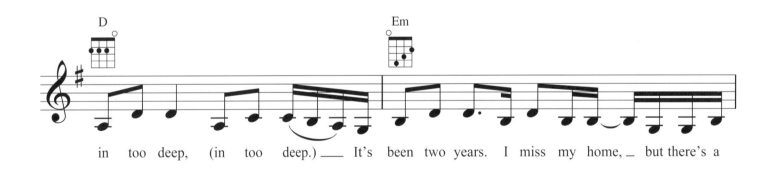

in too deep, (in too deep.) ___ It's been two years. I miss my home, ___ but there's a

fire ___ burn - in' in ___ my bones. ___ I still be - lieve, _____ yeah, I

still   be - lieve. _ And all of those

Coda

I've still got   a lot of fight left in

me, _____

a   lot of fight left   in   me. _____

2. Like a small   boat ____

on the o - cean _

send - ing big   waves ___

in - to mo - tion. _

Like how a sin - gle word ___

can make a heart ___ o -

pen.

I might on - ly have   one match,

27

Love Wins

Words and Music by David Garcia, Brett James and Carrie Underwood

First note

Verse
Moderately slow, in 2

1. Stray bul - let and a ma - ma cries.

Her ba - by won't be com - ing home to - night. Si - rens scream - ing down the

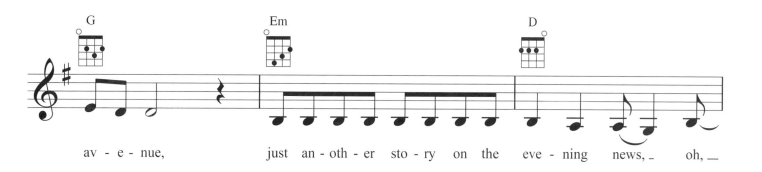

av - e - nue, just an - oth - er sto - ry on the eve - ning news, __ oh, __

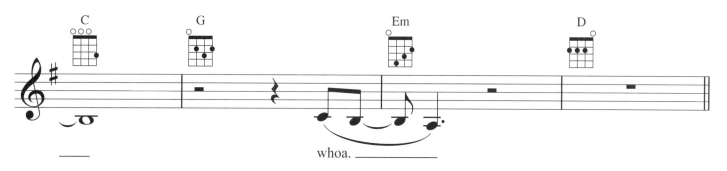

whoa. ____ __

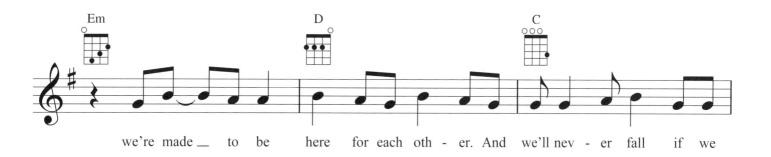

we're made __ to be here for each oth - er. And we'll nev - er fall if we

walk hand in hand, put a world that seems bro - ken to - geth - er a - gain. Yeah,

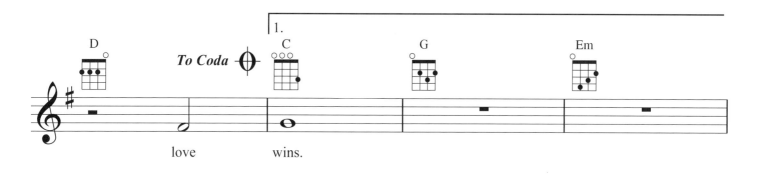

I, _____ I ____ be - lieve in ____ the end,

love wins.

Verse

3. Some - times it takes a lot of faith

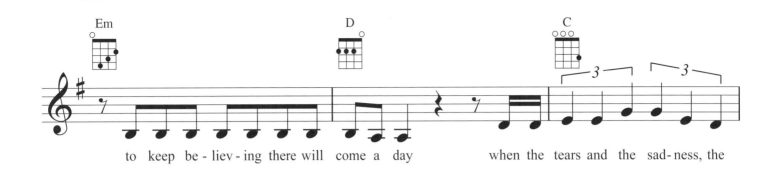

to keep be - liev - ing there will come a day when the tears and the sad - ness, the

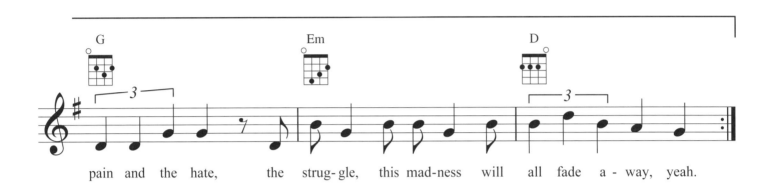

pain and the hate, the strug - gle, this mad - ness will all fade a - way, yeah.

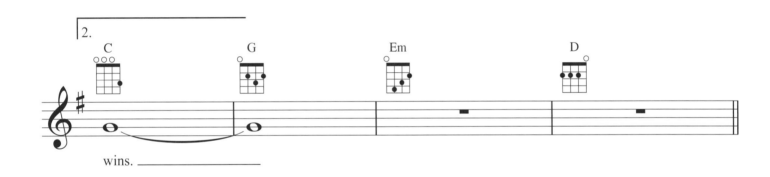

wins.

Bridge

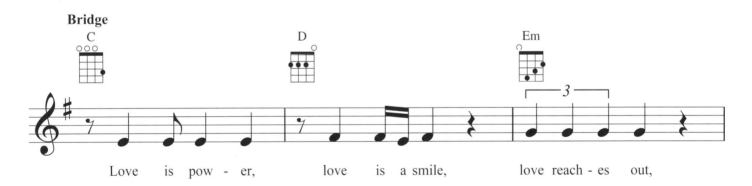

Love is pow - er, love is a smile, love reach - es out,

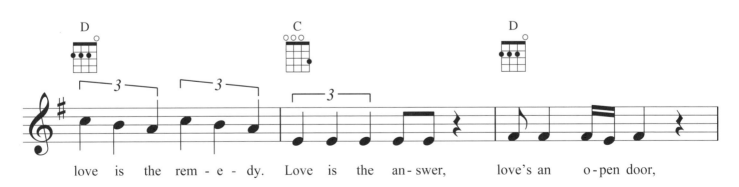

love is the rem - e - dy. Love is the an - swer, love's an o - pen door,

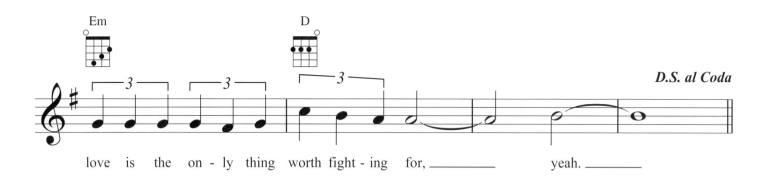

D.S. al Coda

love is the on-ly thing worth fight-ing for, _____ yeah. _____

⊕ Coda

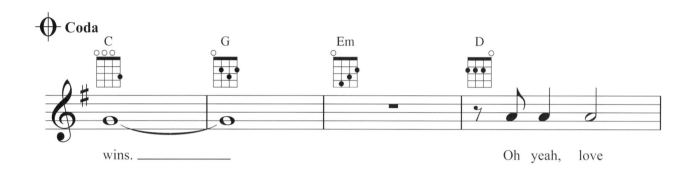

wins. _____ Oh yeah, love

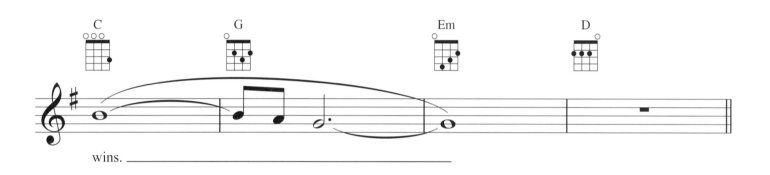

wins. _____

Outro

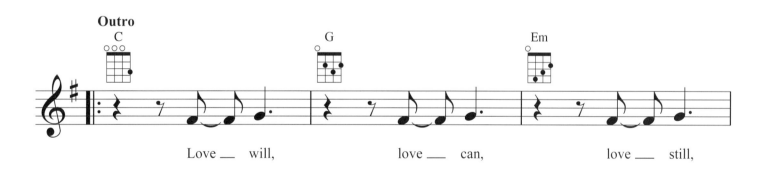

Love __ will, love __ can, love __ still,

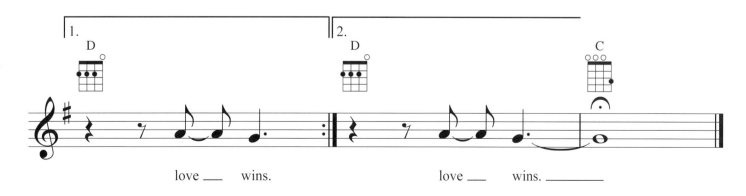

1.
love __ wins.

2.
love __ wins. _____

Home

Words and Music by Greg Holden and Drew Pearson

just know you're

not a - lone, ____ 'cause I'm gon - na

make this place your _____ home.

Verse

Set - tle down, _____

it - 'll all be ____ clear.

Don't pay __ no mind to __ the de - mons; they

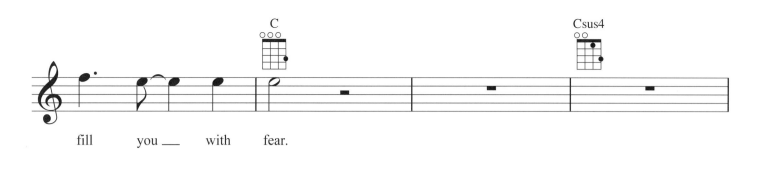

fill   you ___ with   fear.

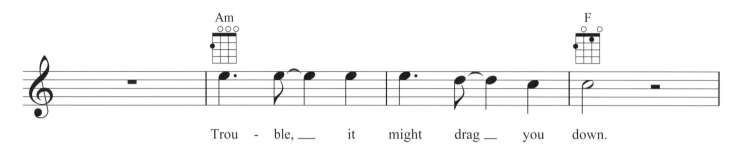

Trou - ble, ___ it   might   drag ___ you   down.

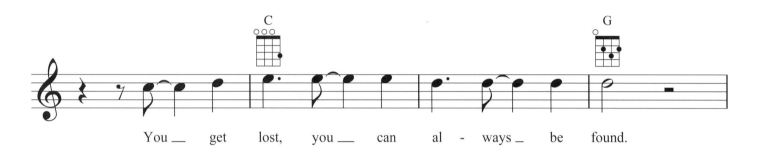

You ___ get   lost,   you ___ can   al - ways ___ be   found.

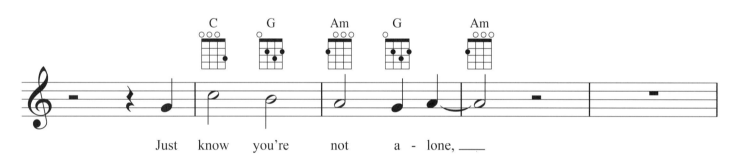

Just   know   you're   not   a - lone, ___

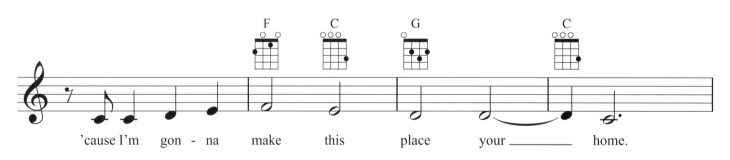

'cause I'm   gon - na   make   this   place   your _____ home.

Interlude

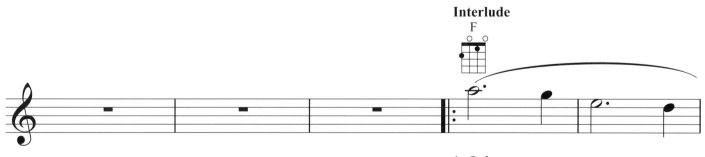

1. Ooh, _____

2.–5. Ah, _____

ooh.

ah.

Ooh.

Ah.

1., 2., 4.

3.　　　　D.S.　5.　Outro

Ah,

ah.

Ah.

I Dare You

Words and Music by Benjamin West, Jeffrey Gitelman,
Natalie Hemby, Laura Veltz and Jesse Shatkin

First note

Moderately

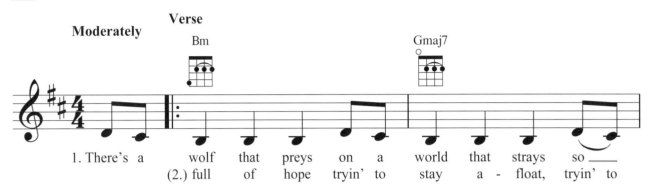

1. There's a wolf that preys on a world that strays so ____
(2.) full of hope tryin' to stay a - float, tryin' to

far from the gar - den.
save one an - oth - er.
And just like your ___ own, ev - 'ry
Peo - ple let you ___ drown 'cause they

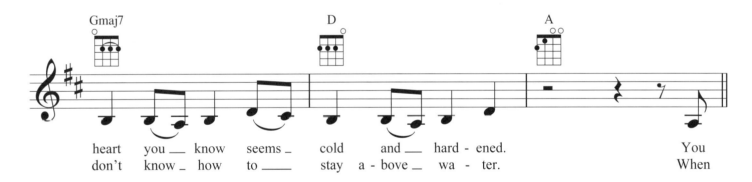

heart you ___ know seems ___ cold and ___ hard - ened.
don't know ___ how to ____ stay a - bove ___ wa - ter.
You
When

Pre-Chorus

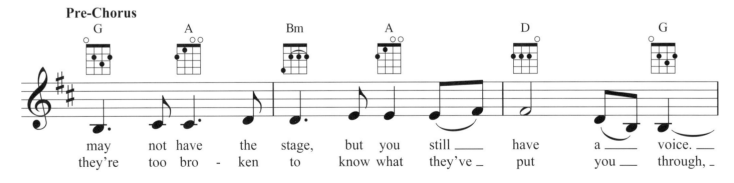

may not have the stage, but you still ____ have a voice. ____
they're too bro - ken to know what they've ___ put you ___ through, ___

Lean on Me

Words and Music by Bill Withers

Em   Dm   F

_____ I'll help you car - ry ___ on; _____

C   C7   F   Dm   C

for   it won't be long _____ 'til I'm gon - na need ___

G   C

_____ some - bod - y to lean _____ on. ___

Verse

C   C7   F   Dm   C

2. Please _____ swal - low your pride _____ if I have things _
3. If _____ there is a load _____ you have to bear _

Em   Dm   F

_____ you need to bor - row, _____
       that you can't car - ry, _____

C   C7   F   Dm   C

for   no one can fill _____ those of your needs _
I'm   right up the road. _____ I'll share your load _

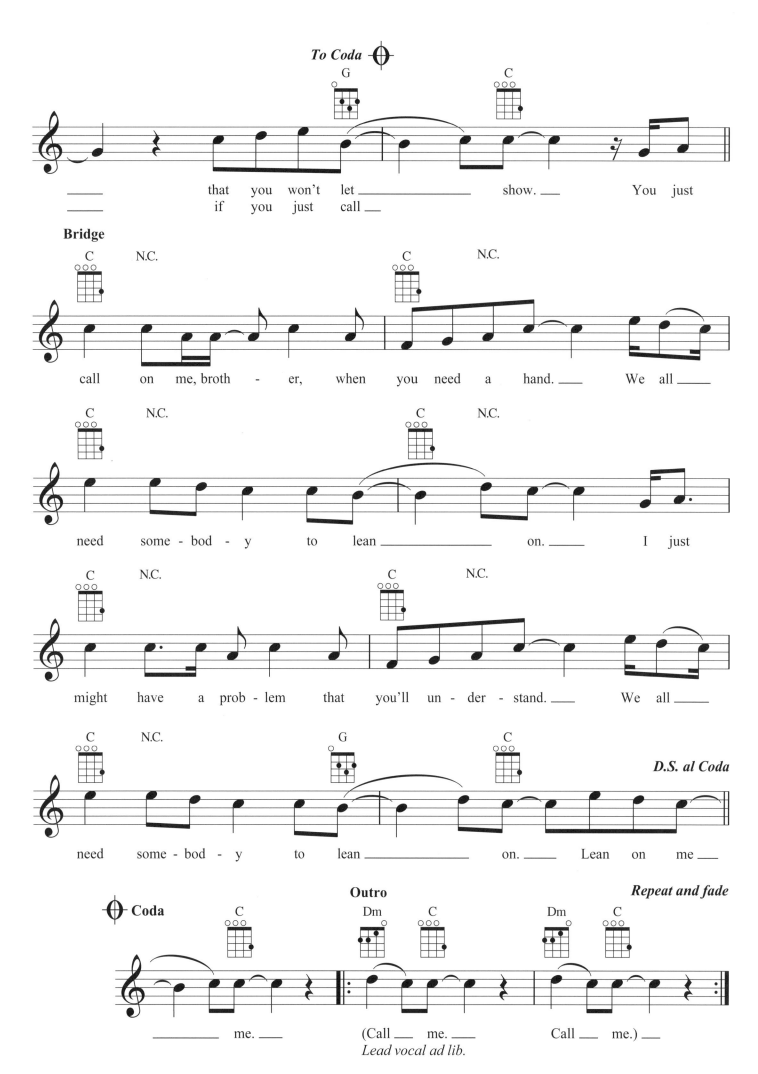

Stand by Me

Words and Music by Jerry Leiber, Mike Stoller and Ben E. King

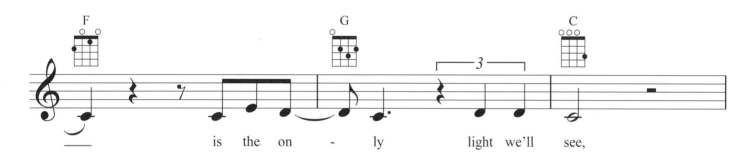

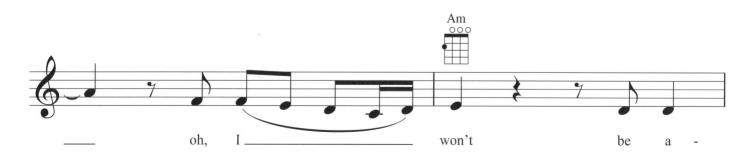

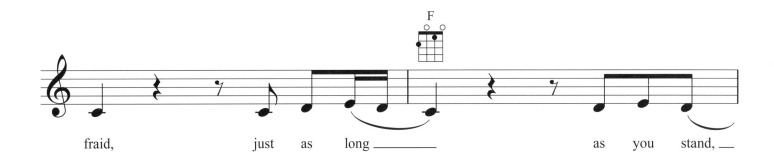

fraid,　　just as long＿＿＿＿　　as you stand, ＿

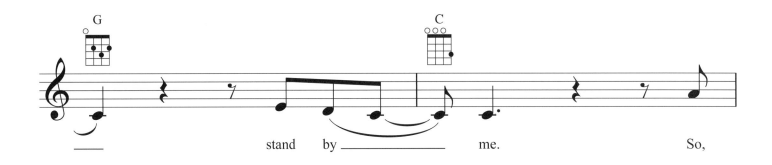

＿　　stand by ＿＿＿＿ me.　　So,

Chorus

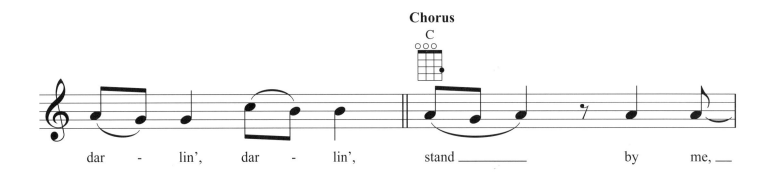

dar - lin', dar - lin', 　stand ＿＿＿＿ by me, ＿

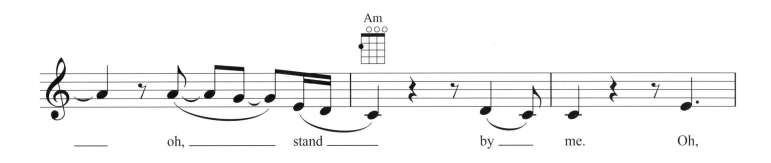

＿　　oh, ＿＿＿ stand ＿＿＿ by ＿ me.　　Oh,

stand, ＿　　　stand by ＿ me, 　　stand by ＿ me.

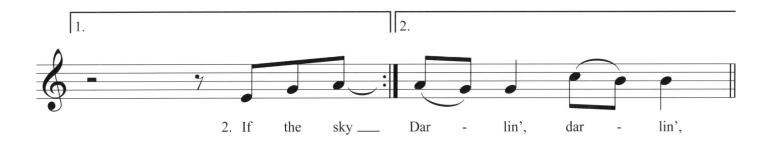

2. If the sky ___ Dar - lin', dar - lin',

Outro-Chorus

C

stand _____ by me, _____ oh, _____ stand _____

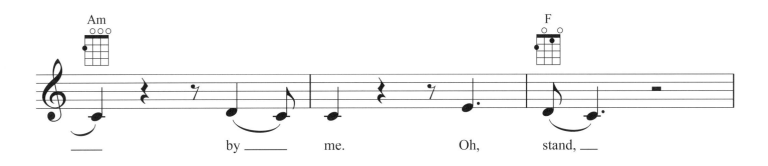

Am   F

___ by ___ me. Oh, stand, ___

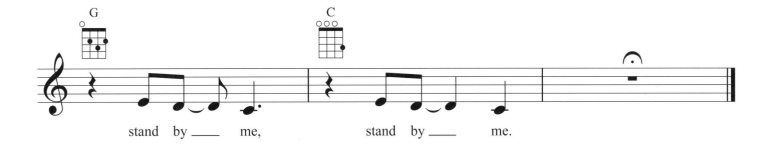

G   C

stand by ___ me, stand by ___ me.

Additional Lyrics

2. If the sky that we look upon should tumble and fall,
   Or the mountains should crumble to the sea,
   I won't cry, I won't cry. No, I won't shed a tear,
   Just as long as you stand, stand by me.
   And darlin', darlin'... (*To Chorus*)

One Call Away

**Words and Music by Charlie Puth, Justin Franks, Breyan Isaac,
Matt Prime, Blake Anthony Carter and Maureen McDonald**

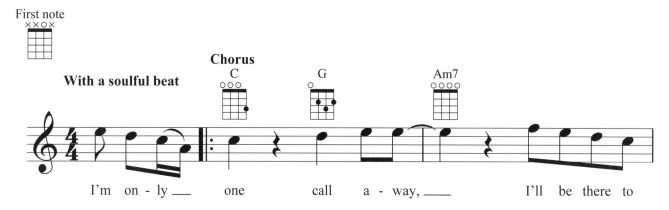

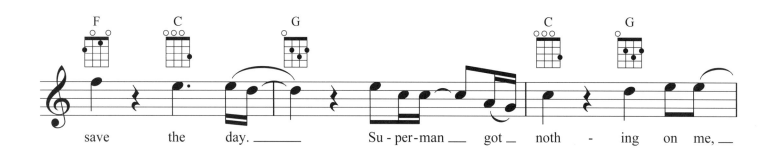

I'm on-ly ___ one call a-way, ___ I'll be there to

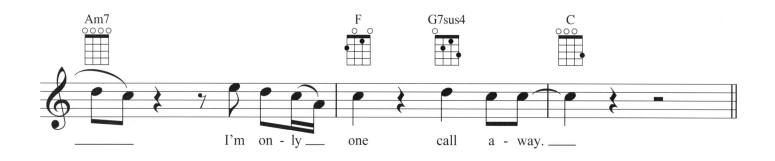

save the day. ___ Su-per-man ___ got ___ noth-ing on me, ___

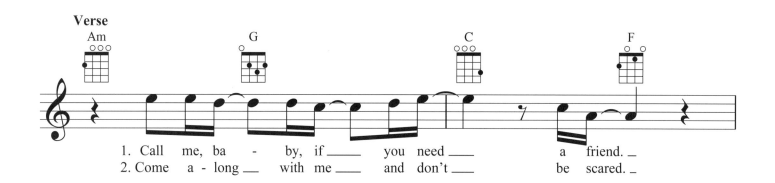

___ I'm on-ly ___ one call a-way. ___

1. Call me, ba - by, if ___ you need ___ a friend. ___
2. Come a - long ___ with me ___ and don't ___ be scared. _

Rise Up

Words and Music by Cassandra Batie and Jennifer Decilveo

First note

Moderately slow, in 2

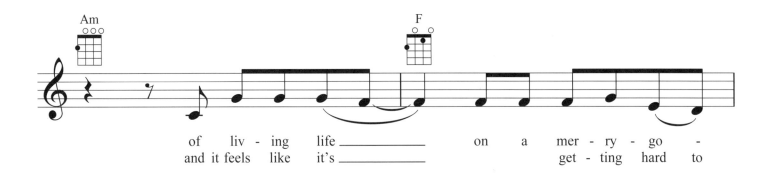

1. You're bro - ken down and _____ ti - red
2. When the si - lence is - n't _____ qui - et

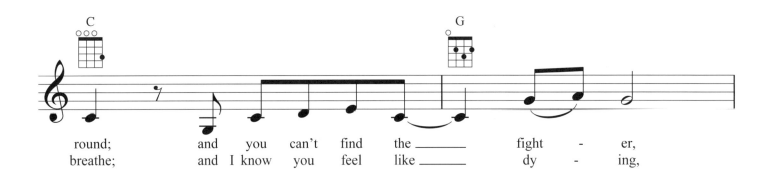

of liv - ing life _____ on a mer - ry - go -
and it feels like it's _____ get - ting hard to

round;   and you can't find the _____ fight - er,
breathe;   and I know you feel like _____ dy - ing,

but I see it in you, ___ so we gon' walk it out.   Move _____
but I prom - ise we'll _____ take the world to its feet.   Move _____

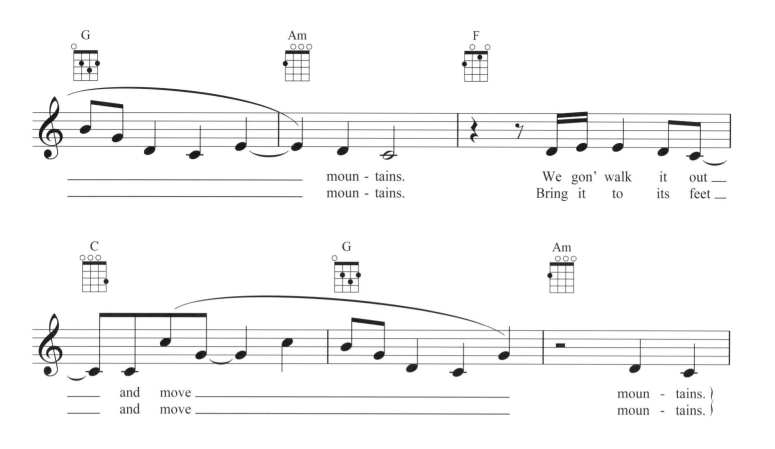

moun - tains. We gon' walk it out __
moun - tains. Bring it to its feet __

__ and move _____ moun - tains. }
__ and move _____ moun - tains. }

Chorus

And I'll rise ____ up, I'll rise ____ like the day. __ I'll rise _

__ up, I'll rise ____ un - a - fraid. __ I'll rise ____ up and

To Coda ⊕

I'll do it a thou - sand ____ times a - gain. And I'll rise _

_____ up high _____ like the waves. _ I'll rise _____ up in spite _

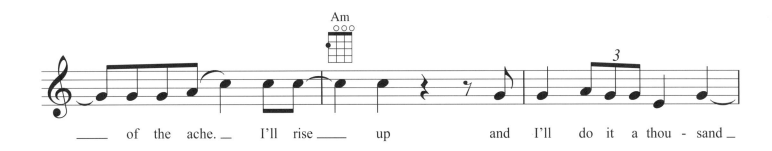

_____ of the ache. _ I'll rise _____ up and I'll do it a thou - sand _

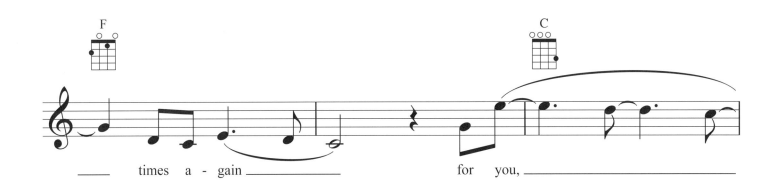

_____ times a - gain _____ for you, _____

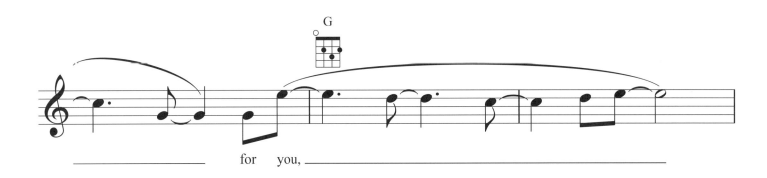

_____ for you, _____

D.C. al Coda

you, _____ for you. _____

Coda

_____ times a - gain _____ for you, _____

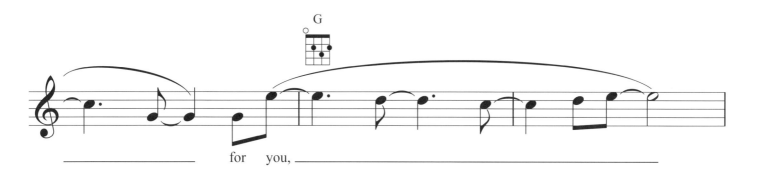

_____ for you, _____

you, _____ for you. _____

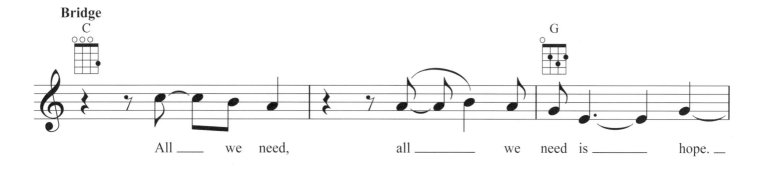

Bridge

All ____ we need, all _____ we need is _____ hope. __

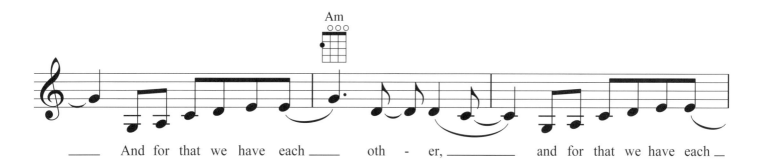

_____ And for that we have each ____ oth - er, _____ and for that we have each __

____ oth - er. And   we ____ will rise,   we ____ will rise,

we'll _ rise ____ up. ____

We'll ____ rise. ____   I'll rise ____

Chorus

____ up,   rise ____ like the day. ____ I'll rise up   in ____

spite of the ache.   I will rise   a thou - sand times ____

____ a - gain. ____   And we'll rise ____ up   high ____

like the waves. _ We'll rise ___ up in spite _ of the ache. _ We'll rise _

___ up and we'll do it a thou-sand ___ times a-gain ____

_ for you, _____ for you, _

_____ you, _____ for you. _

Outro

_____ (Hm, hm, ___

hm, _____ hm.) ____

57

Tomorrow

from the Musical Production ANNIE
Lyric by Martin Charnin
Music by Charles Strouse

First note

Chorus
Moderately slow

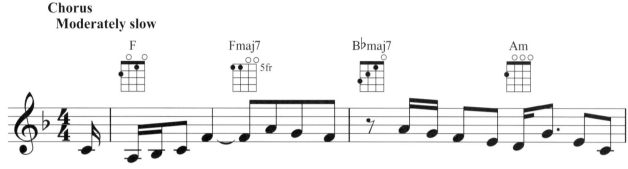

The sun-'ll come out ___ to-mor-row, bet your bot-tom dol-lar that to-

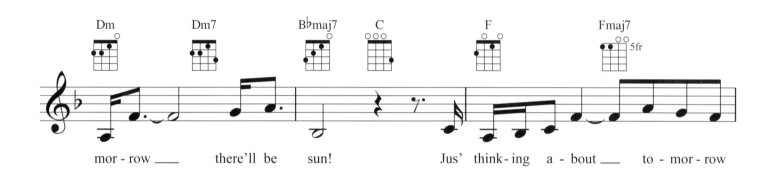

mor-row ___ there'll be sun! Jus' think-ing a-bout ___ to-mor-row

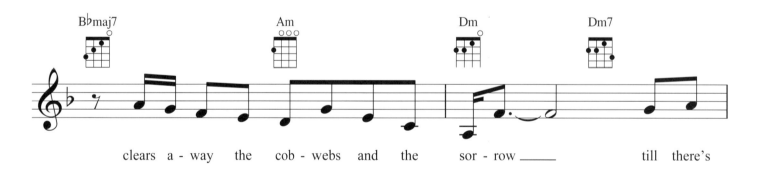

clears a-way the cob-webs and the sor-row ___ till there's

Bridge

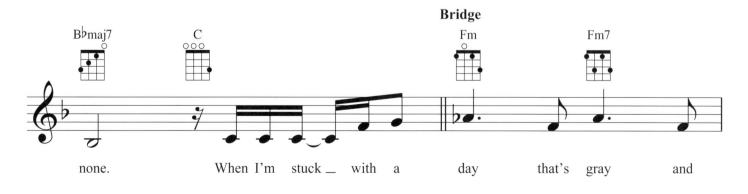

none. When I'm stuck ___ with a day that's gray and

lone - ly,   I just stick ___ out my chin and grin and

Chorus

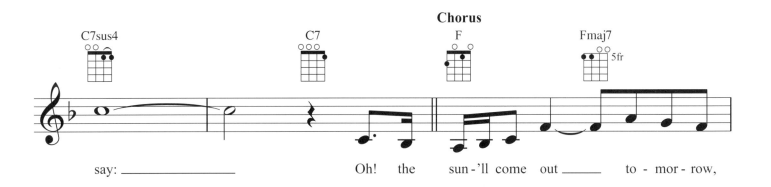

say: _____   Oh! the sun -'ll come out _____ to - mor - row,

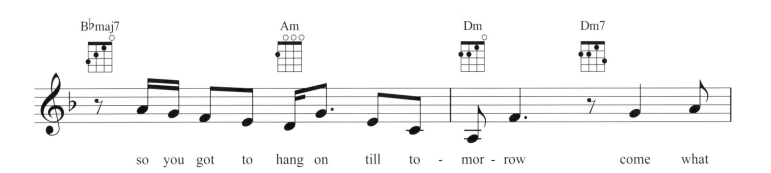

so you got to hang on till to - mor - row   come what

Outro

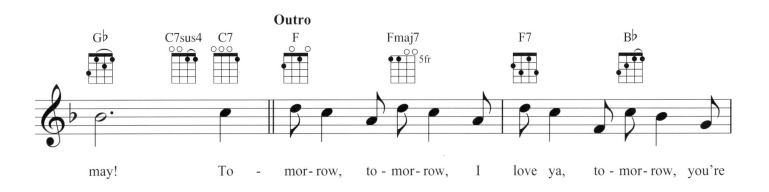

may!   To - mor - row, to - mor - row, I love ya, to - mor - row, you're

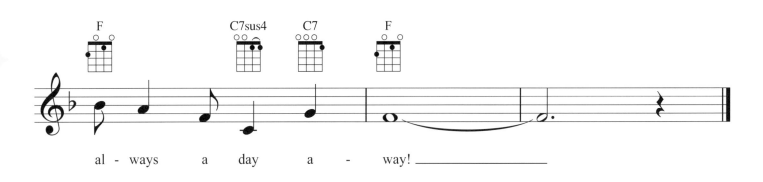

al - ways a day a - way! _____

Underdog

Words and Music by Alicia Augello-Cook, Ed Sheeran,
Amy Wadge, Foy Vance, Jonny Coffer and Johnny McDaid

teach - ers, stu - dent doc - tors, sons on the front line know-ing they don't

get to run. ___ This ___ goes out ___ to the un - der- dog: Keep ___

___ on keep - ing at what you love, and you'll find that some - day,

soon e - nough, you will rise up, rise ___ up, yeah. ___

Interlude

(Instrumental)

To Coda

2. She's rid - ing in a

Verse

tax - i back to the kitch - en, talk - ing to the driv - er 'bout his wife and his chil -

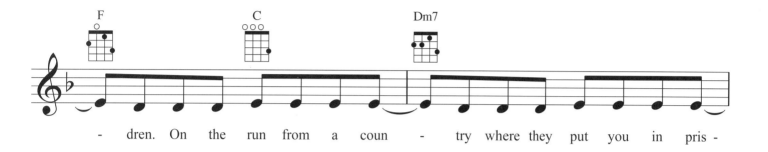

- dren. On the run from a coun - try where they put you in pris -

D.S. al Coda

- on for be - ing a wom - an and speak - ing your mind. ___ And she looked in his

Coda   **Bridge**

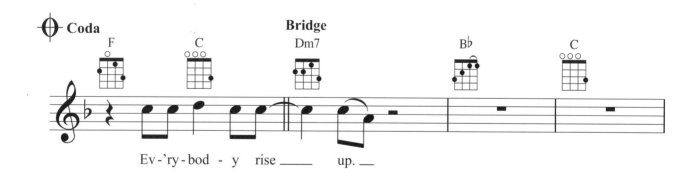

Ev - 'ry - bod - y rise ___ up. ___

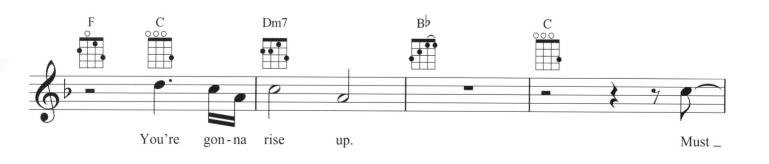

You're gon - na rise up.   Must _

Outro-Chorus

(Hus - tlers wait - ing at the bus stop, _ sing a song for the hus - tlers. *(Lead vocal ad lib.)* moth - ers wait - ing on a check to come, _ young teach - ers, stu - dent doc - tors, sons on the front line know - ing they don't get to run.) _ This _ _ goes out _ to the un - der - dog: Keep _ on keep - ing at what you love, and you'll find that some - day, soon e - nough, you will rise up, rise _ up, yeah. _

We're All in This Together

from HIGH SCHOOL MUSICAL
Words and Music by Matthew Gerrard and Robbie Nevil

⊕ **Coda**

Pre-Chorus

Female: We've ar - rived __ be - cause we stuck to - geth - er, cham - pi-ons one and all. __

Chorus

_____ *All:* We're all in this __ to - geth - er; once __ we know __

all in this __ to - geth - er, when __ we reach, __

__ that we are, __ we're all stars, __ and we see __ that. We're all in this __ to - geth -

__ we can fly, __ know in - side __ we can make __ it. We're all in this __ to - geth -

1.

- er, and __ it shows __ when we stand __ hand in hand, __ make our dreams __ come... We're

- er; once __ we see _____ there's a chance __ that we have __

2. **Outro**

__ and we take __ it. Wild - cats ev - 'ry - where, wave your hands up in the air.

That's the way we do it; let's get to it, c' - mon, __ ev - 'ry - one! __

We Are Warriors
(Warrior)

Words and Music by Avril Lavigne, Chad Kroeger and Travis Clark

First note

Verse
Moderately slow

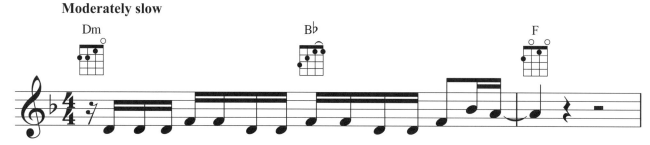

1. We'll pick our bat - tles 'cause we know we're gon - na win the war. ____
2. Like __ vik - ings, we'll be fight - ing through the day and night. ____

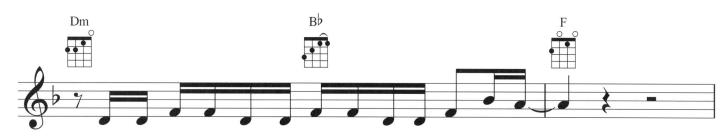

We're not rat - tled 'cause we shat - tered all of this be - fore. ____
We'll be march - ing through the dark - ness till the morn - ing lights. ____

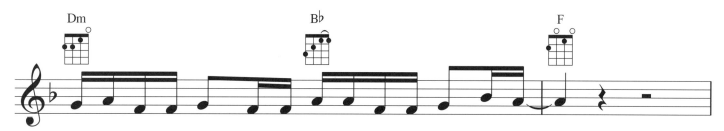

Stead - i - er than steel 'cause we're read - y with our shield and sword. ____
E - ven when it's hard - er, like the ar - mor, you will see us shine. ____

Back on the sad - dle 'cause we've gath - ered all our strength for more. ____ And
No, we won't stop and we won't drop un - til the vic - to - ry's ours. ____ No,

With a Little Help from My Friends

Words and Music by John Lennon and Paul McCartney

Verse
Moderate Swing feel

1. What would you do _____ if I sang _____
2. What do I do _____ when my love _____
3. (Would you be - lieve _____ in a love _____

_____ out of tune? _____ Would you stand _____ up and walk _____ out on me? _____
_____ is a - way? _____ (Does it wor - ry you to be a - lone?) _____
_____ at first sight?) _____ Yes, I'm cer - tain that it hap - pens all the

_____ time.
Lend me your ears _____ and I'll sing _____
How do I feel _____ by the end _____
(What do you see _____ when you turn _____

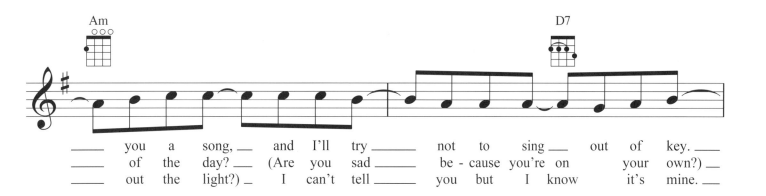

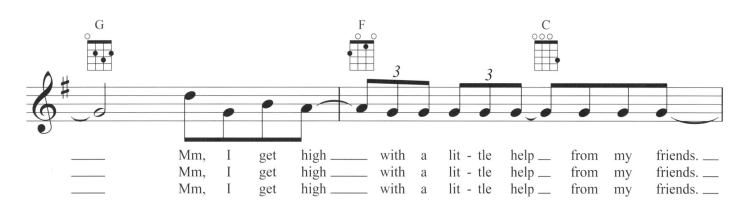

Chorus

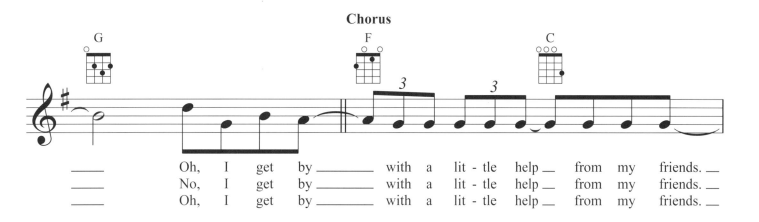

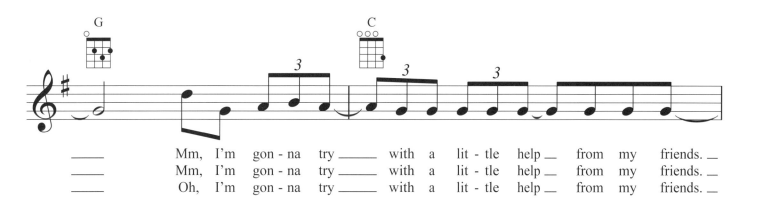

Mm, I'm gon-na try ___ with a lit-tle help ___ from my friends. ___

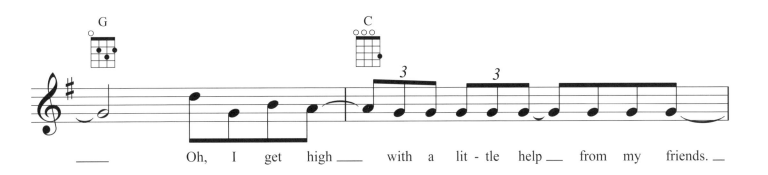

Oh, I get high ___ with a lit-tle help ___ from my friends. ___

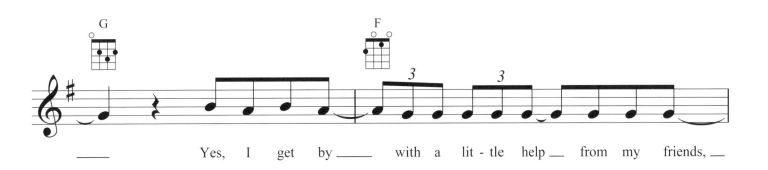

Yes, I get by ___ with a lit-tle help ___ from my friends, ___

with a lit-tle help ___ from my friends. ___

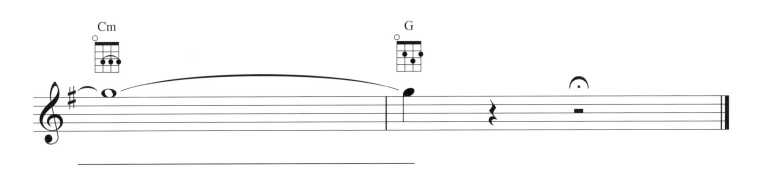

You Will Be Found

from DEAR EVAN HANSEN

Music and Lyrics by Benj Pasek and Justin Paul

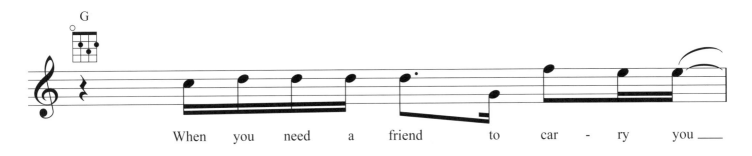

When you need a friend to car - ry you _____

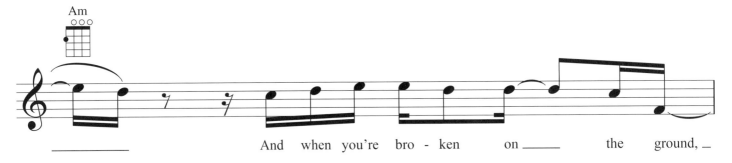

_____ And when you're bro - ken on _____ the ground, _

A tempo

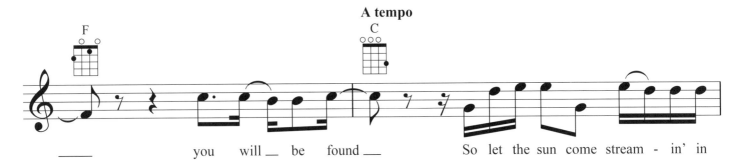

_____ you will _ be found _ So let the sun come stream - in' in

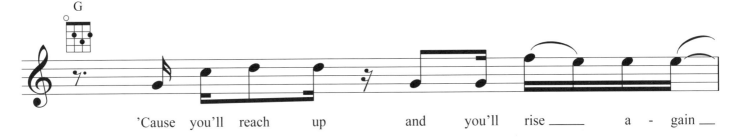

'Cause you'll reach up and you'll rise _____ a - gain _

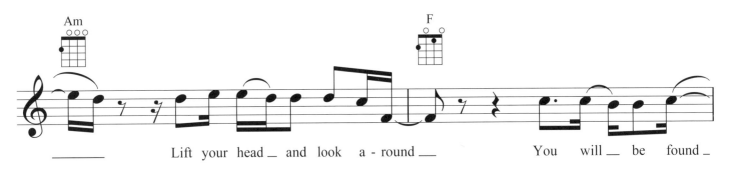

_____ Lift your head _ and look a - round _ You will _ be found _

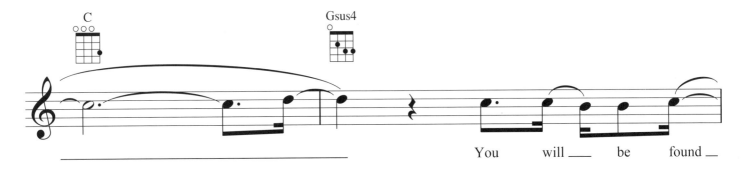

_____ You will _ be found _

You will __ be found __

You will __ be __ found __

You __ will be _____ found __

Interlude

ALANA: *Have you seen this? Someone put a video of your speech online.*
EVAN: *My speech?*

ALANA: *People started sharing it, I guess, and now,*
I mean, Connor is everywhere.
JARED: *Your speech is everywhere.*

JARED: (con't) *This morning, the Connor Project page,*
it had fifty-six people following it.
EVAN: *How many does it have now?*
JARED: *Four thousand, five hundred, and eighty-two.*

CYNTHIA: (overlapping with **JARED**):
Sixteen thousand, two hundred,
and thirty-nine.

You've Got a Friend

Words and Music by Carole King

Additional Lyrics

2. If the sky above you should turn dark and full of clouds
   And that old North wind should begin to blow,
   Keep your head together and call my name out loud, now.
   Soon I'll be knockin' upon your door.

You'll Never Walk Alone

from CAROUSEL
Lyrics by Oscar Hammerstein II
Music by Richard Rodgers

The Best Collections for Ukulele

The Best Songs Ever

70 songs have now been arranged for ukulele. Includes: Always • Bohemian Rhapsody • Memory • My Favorite Things • Over the Rainbow • Piano Man • What a Wonderful World • Yesterday • You Raise Me Up • and more.

00282413 . . . . $17.99

Campfire Songs for Ukulele

30 favorites to sing as you roast marshmallows and strum your uke around the campfire. Includes: God Bless the U.S.A. • Hallelujah • The House of the Rising Sun • I Walk the Line • Puff the Magic Dragon • Wagon Wheel • You Are My Sunshine • and more.

00129170 . . . . $14.99

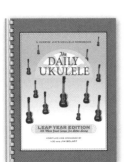

The Daily Ukulele

compiled and arranged by

Liz and Jim Beloff
Strum a different song everyday with easy arrangements of 365 of your favorite songs in one big songbook! Includes favorites by the Beatles, Beach Boys, and Bob Dylan, folk songs, pop songs, kids' songs, Christmas carols, and Broadway and Hollywood tunes, all with a spiral binding for ease of use.

00240356 . . . . $39.99

The Daily Ukulele – Leap Year Edition

366 More Songs for Better Living

compiled and arranged by Liz and Jim Beloff
An amazing second volume with 366 MORE songs for you to master each day of a leap year! Includes: Ain't No Sunshine • Calendar Girl • I Got You Babe • Lean on Me • Moondance • and many, many more.

00240681 . . . . $39.99

Disney Hits for Ukulele

Play 23 of your favorite Disney songs on your ukulele. Includes: The Bare Necessities • Cruella De Vil • Do You Want to Build a Snowman? • Kiss the Girl • Lava • Let It Go • Once upon a Dream • A Whole New World • and more.

00151250 . . . . $14.99

First 50 Songs You Should Play on Ukulele

An amazing collection of 50 accessible, must-know favorites: Edelweiss • Hey, Soul Sister • I Walk the Line • I'm Yours • Imagine • Over the Rainbow • Peaceful Easy Feeling • The Rainbow Connection • Riptide • and many more.

00149250 . . . . $14.99

The Ukulele 4 Chord Songbook

With just 4 chords, you can play 50 hot songs on your ukulele! Songs include: Brown Eyed Girl • Do Wah Diddy Diddy • Hey Ya! • Ho Hey • Jessie's Girl • Let It Be • One Love • Stand by Me • Toes • With or Without You • and many more.

00142050 . . . . $16.99

Simple Songs for Ukulele

50 favorites for standard G-C-E-A ukulele tuning, including: All Along the Watchtower • Can't Help Falling in Love • Don't Worry, Be Happy • Ho Hey • I'm Yours • King of the Road • Sweet Home Alabama • You Are My Sunshine • and more.

00156815 . . . . $14.99

Top Hits of 2019

Strum your favorite songs of 2019 on the uke! Includes: Bad Guy (Billie Eilish) • I Don't Care (Ed Sheeran & Justin Bieber) • ME! (Taylor Swift) • Old Town Road (Remix) (Lil Nas X feat. Billy Ray Cyrus) • Senorita (Shawn Mendes & Camila Cabello) • Someone You Loved (Lewis Capaldi) • and more.

00302274 . . . . $14.99

The Ukulele 3 Chord Songbook

If you know three chords, you can play these 50 great hits! Songs include: Bad Moon Rising • A Boy Named Sue • King of the Road • Leaving on a Jet Plane • Shelter from the Storm • Time for Me to Fly • Twist and Shout • and many more.

00141143 . . . . $16.99

The Ultimate Ukulele Fake Book

Uke enthusiasts will love this giant, spiral-bound collection of over 400 songs for uke! Includes: Crazy • Dancing Queen • Downtown • Fields of Gold • Happy • Hey Jude • 7 Years • Summertime • Thinking Out Loud • Thriller • Wagon Wheel • and more.

00175500 . . . . $45.00

Ukulele – The Most Requested Songs

Strum & Sing Series

Cherry Lane Music
Nearly 50 favorites all expertly arranged for ukulele! Includes: Bubbly • Build Me Up Buttercup • Cecilia • Georgia on My Mind • Kokomo • L-O-V-E • Your Body Is a Wonderland • and dozens more.

02501453 . . . . $14.99

HAL•LEONARD®

02
4